NOTES ON SEAFORD,

HISTORICAL, ANTIQUARIAN, ANECDOTICAL, AND DESCRIPTIVE.

BY

MARK ANTONY LOWER, M.A., F.S.A.,

ETC.

LEWES: G. P. BACON.

1868

In the interest of creating a more extensive selection of rare historical book reprints, we have chosen to reproduce this title even though it may possibly have occasional imperfections such as missing and blurred pages, missing text, poor pictures, markings, dark backgrounds and other reproduction issues beyond our control. Because this work is culturally important, we have made it available as a part of our commitment to protecting, preserving and promoting the world's literature. Thank you for your understanding.

Seaside Education, Seaford, Sussex.

59 Miles by Railway, S. of London.

Mr. Mark Antony Lower, M.A., F.S.A.,

Author of "Patronymica Britannica," "English Surnames," "Curiosities of Heraldry," Translator of the "Chronicon de Bello," &c. &c. &c.,

Receives into his care *two or three* Pupils to prepare for the various examinations, and for active life in its several departments.

Seaford offers every facility for Sea Bathing, and careful Medical treatment. Gentlemen whose early education has been imperfect will find with Mr. Lower the advantages of a strict educational oversight, combined with those of a comfortable home.

References to many gentlemen of high literary attainments and social position.

Terms, 100 and 120 Guineas
Per Annum, payable Quarterly.

NOTES ON SEAFORD.

A HANDBOOK FOR VISITORS.

BRIGHTON—Queen of Watering-Places—Hastings, Scarborough, Torquay, Ramsgate, Ryde, Dawlish, St. Leonards, Weston-super-Mare, Worthing, Eastbourne, Llandudno, Margate, will please to keep silence while I rehearse the manifold advantages of this little sea-side resort, remarkable for the salubrity of its climate, the romantic beauty of its scenery,[*] the quietness of its surroundings, the snug comfort of its simple lodgings, and the civility of its tradesmen. It possesses none of the glitter and glare of more fashionable resorts; there are no splendid equipages in its streets; no long lists of fashionable arrivals in the newspapers; no grand libraries and lounging-rooms; no ceremonious introductions; nothing, in short, that need interfere with the perfect calm which is the desideratum of the overworked student, the valetudinarian, the quiet observer of the beauties of nature, the geologist, the sea-angler, the pedestrian, or the lover of horse exercise on the free open down. The great Wellington has visited it, and it was here that Tennyson wrote his

[*] A loyal tradesman of Seaford lately assured a friend of mine that the town was "*allowed* to be one of the most healthiest and picture-skue places any-where!"

Funeral Ode on that mighty hero. The great names of William Pitt (afterwards Lord Chatham) and George Canning have been politically associated with it,* and many persons of eminence in law, literature, science, the navy, the army, and commerce, have sought shelter in this quiet retreat from the busy hum of great cities; and although they have had here neither paternal acres, nor oxen to till them withal, have been able to realize to some extent, for awhile, the

"Beatus ille qui procul negotiis,
Ut prisca gens mortalium,".

of the Roman poet.

Seaford is not destitute, however, of the appliances of modern civilization. It has, in carpenter's phrase, "two posts and a rail"—in other words, railway communication with the metropolis in little more than two hours, and with every part of the south of England; and two deliveries of letters daily. The great Babylon of watering-places—Brighton—is within a fifty minutes' journey by the South Coast Railway, and Lewes, the county-town of Sussex, within twenty-five minutes; so that should the visitor have occasion to relieve the comparative solitude of this little sea-side place, he can do so with great facility and at trifling cost. A still further variety may be obtained by an occasional trip across the Channel from Newhaven—a port three miles westward—to Dieppe, a voyage of sixty-four miles, which is usually accomplished in five or six hours.

Seaford (in the vernacular of its fishermen, *Saifoord,* in the speech of strangers, Seafŏrd, and in that of strict propriety,

* It had also the doubtful honour of being 'owned' by Thomas Pelham, the great political Duke of Newcastle, who had a large mansion at Bishopston, close by.

Sĕafŏrd, with equal *ictus* on both its syllables, as if it were two words) is a very ancient place. It probably derived its name from some small colony of Norsemen, a thousand years ago, the words *Sae Fiord* in their ancient tongue signifying "The Bay," which is a good geographical denotement of its situation on the indent of the English Channel known as Seaford Bay.*

Let us fix the exact geographical position of this interesting old town. It lies, then, locally within the hundred of Flexborough, rape of Pevensey, county of Sussex, and is, in a straight line, thirteen miles east of Brighton, and by rail fifty-nine miles almost due south of London. The town stands near the eastern end of the Bay to which it gives, or rather from which, etymologically, it takes, its name. This bay extends from Newhaven Heights on the west, to Cliff End on the east, and, measured at its base, is about three miles in length. The interval between the two masses of South Down hills is chiefly composed of a rich alluvial soil, the former bed and delta of the river Ouse, which, rising in the Weald of Sussex, assumed, near Lewes, the proportions of a considerable estuary, varying in breadth from a quarter of a mile to a mile. The original outlet of this river was at the western verge of Seaford Bay, where it was commanded by important earthworks, traces of which are still discernible on Newhaven Heights. From this point ran the Roman road, known as the "Ermin Street," which passed through the counties of

---

* It may be a fanciful conclusion of mine; but I think I see in the complexion and in the general *physique* of the Seaford sea-goers a good deal of the Norseman. The great frequency of the name of Simmons (*olim* Seaman or Seman) shows the maritime pursuits of the olden inhabitants. This name is found in a Subsidy-Roll as early as 1296.

Sussex and Surrey to the metropolis. The prevalence of south-west winds and heavy tides on this part of the coast, however, choked up the natural and proper outlet of the river by hurling up vast beds of shingle, and so driving the current of fresh water three miles eastward to Seaford, where, as it encountered a sturdy cliff, it was compelled to force its way into the English Channel. Hence the *port* of Seaford, which became in course of time a place of some commercial importance, as we shall see hereafter. Almost three centuries ago, by the application of such engineering skill as was then available, the marshes were drained, and sea-defences established at the west end of the bay, so that the Ouse was made to return to its ancient outlet near the village of Meeching, which thenceforward assumed the name of "the New Haven,"[*] and Seaford lost its former importance.

The parish of Seaford contains about 2,280 acres of land. As it lies principally on the South Downs, the subsoil is generally chalk. The herbage is of a kind well adapted to the rearing of sheep. Wheat, barley, and other crops, both cereal and green, flourish abundantly. The parish is bounded on the east by the river Cuckmere, on the north by Alfriston, on the north-west and west by Blatchington, and on the south by the English Channel. The principal proprietors of lands and houses are the Earl of Chichester, Mrs. Major Harison, Lord Howard de Walden and Seaford, Dr. Tyler Smith, the Chambers family, John Purcell Fitzgerald, Esq., Thomas Crook, Esq., and William Allfrey, Esq.

The population of Seaford, as returned by the census of

[*] In contradistinction to the *New*-Haven, the closed outlet of the river at Seaford was known as the *Old* Haven, and a field close by was called the *West* Haven.

1801 was 847; in 1811, 1,001; in 1821, 1,047; in 1831, 1,098. In 1841 it sank to 953; in 1851 it was 997, and in 1861 it rose to 1,085. Within the last seven years there has been a gradual increase to between 1,200 and 1,300, exclusive of visitors, who during the "season," when every available house and cottage are occupied, make the total about 1,500. The number of houses at the last census was about 200, but several building speculations having been set on foot, that number has considerably increased.

Few places on the southern coast are more agreeably situated. Though the lower portion of the town is exposed in the winter months to winds from the south and southwest, Seaford is sheltered by bold eminences from the North and East winds. The sea view is romantic and pleasing. The bay, with its bold sweep, between the heights of Newhaven on the west and those of Seaford Cliff on the east, presents a spectacle of great beauty, especially during the prevalence of an easterly wind, when it is often literally studded with vessels of various sizes and nations, unable to make their way round the dangerous promontory of Beachy Head, about six miles eastward. As many as two hundred sail have been known to be thus detained for days together. On this account Seaford Bay has been named as an eligible point for a breakwater and a harbour of refuge, in connection with Newhaven as a port of outfit and repair. Plans and particulars for such a scheme were published by authority, in 1845, and the estimated cost was £1,250,000. More recently, a plan on a much more extensive scale has been projected.

For *salubrity*, scarcely a spot on the southern coast can

vie with Seaford. The longevity of the inhabitants is proverbial. Fourscore is a very common age; ninety is very far from rare: 'Old' John Banks died in 1854, at the patriarchal age of ninety-nine. A friend of the writer met him one day and promised him a guinea if he lived to be a hundred. "I'll try," said the worthy old man, but he succumbed to the last enemy four months before he had completed the century. His son, 'Young' John Banks, was then a vigorous lad closely verging on fourscore! but he too is now numbered with the things of the past. For the following account of the natural advantages and the prospective improvements of Seaford I am indebted to a friend who has long studied the subject attentively.

It is only during the last few years that Seaford has been known and frequented as a health resort. A few words may be said of its climate in summer and in winter. The whole of the town is built on chalk or sand, so that it is rarely, if ever, damp; the soil and the undulating character of the ground render the watershed so perfect, that the town is soon dry again after the heaviest rain. A wet day at Seaford is very rare. Newhaven cliffs and Seaford heights attract the moisture-laden clouds, and they thus pass inland to deposit their burden. The main characteristic of Seaford is the Bay, which, from the depth of water in it, is generally in motion; a perfect calm being a rare condition. The next is the Southdowns, which here descend almost to the water's edge. These magnificent chalk hills, covered by short, elastic, and sweet-scented verdure, are, for the most part, without tree or fence in their wide expanse. In no place in England can sun and wind have freer action. Sometimes visitors complain of the want of shade, and long for the relief to the eyes which trees afford; but the heat is seldom so oppressive at Seaford as it often is in more shaded localities. We are never without a breeze sufficient to fan away the otherwise oppressive heat. Those who study Hygeine, know that free Actination, or exposure to the sun's rays, is one of the most essential causes of health. Human beings and flowers require the sun in this climate for perfection of developement. However pleasant to the eye a wooded district may be, it tells a tale of clay soil and inevitable damp. Not that we would ignore the beauty of trees—and we believe the steep sides of our Southdown hills might be planted with larch and fir in the Scotch fashion, with very fine effect; indeed, the Southdowns might be made in this way one of the most beautiful and attractive districts in the kingdom. Should the hill sides and the denes ever be planted, and the number of trees in and about the town considerably increased, it is to be hoped the broad expanses of the Downs may always remain free and open as at present.

As regards position and climate, Seaford possesses great advantages. It fronts to the south-west, and the most violent of the south-westerly gales are never very cold; it is sheltered on the east by the high range of hills ending in Beachy Head; and to the north by the Southdown range of hills, which here reach a great elevation at the north part of the ridge. The violence of the westerly gales is considerably broken by the Newhaven cliffs. In the coldest day in winter, there is at least the difference of a greatcoat in the temperature, even in an east wind, under our cliffs, as compared with more exposed places. When the wind is from the north, the sea is always calm and tranquil, and the temperature comparatively high on the beach below the "full" or shingle bank. According to the building plans, houses will be erected in the shelter of the hill towards the Cliff-end; which is, we believe, to be called the Undercliff. When this is the case, Seaford will offer as good a shelter to the pulmonary invalid as can be found in this country. As a proof of its mildness, we may mention that swallows have been known to leave us in November, and return again early in April; so that we are only four months of the year without these summer visitors. One great advantage of Seaford is, that in winter the sun sets in the ocean, so that we have the longest possible amount of daylight in the darker months of the year. In any part of Seaford, visitors in delicate health may take a walk in winter, choosing westerly or southerly aspects, according as the wind is from the north or east. Direct exposure to the latter should, of course, always be avoided here as well as elsewhere, on account of its irritating and dry condition.

As regards sanitary statistics, Seaford is in the Eastbourne Union, and the Registration of its Births and Deaths is always included in that of Eastbourne. When we hear the healthiness of Eastbourne spoken of—and it has become proverbial—it should always be remembered that it should be, Eastbourne and Seaford. The Eastbourne district is proved by the Registrar-General's reports to be the healthiest seaside district in England; and in this district Seaford is, as we have said, included. It may be dwelt on with pride, that Seaford does not supply the least satisfactory quota to the figures offered by the Eastbourne district as a whole. Some few years since, the Registrar-General published an account of the mortality occurring in Seaford, on an average of ten years, and it was found that the deaths during the year had been 14 and a fraction per thousand, or less than 1½ per cent.; an unprecedentedly low death-rate. It should be remembered that the vital statistics of the Registrar-General can never be quite fairly stated. They are, of course, based on the decennial census which is taken in the early part of the month of April. This is the time of the year when seaside watering places have a smaller population than at any other time. A place like Seaford, for instance, has nearly double the population in June,

July, August, September, and October, as compared with April. Yet no allowance is made for this, the calculation being made always upon the smaller number instead of—as it should be—upon the mean average population throughout the year. A fair consideration of this element would show the healthiness of sea-side watering places like Seaford and Eastbourne to be even far greater than appears on the face of the sanitary reports. If Seaford has hitherto been highly distinguished for salubrity, it may fairly be expected to vie with any place in the kingdom, now that the drainage has been rendered as perfect as modern sanitary and engineering science can make it. For all invalids requiring a pure, bracing air, with the warmth and sun of a south-western aspect, no place on the south coast has greater advantages. Its quiet and its nearness to London, must make it more and more a favourite resort for residents, and for those requiring holiday relaxation or change of air. Seaford is, in fact, nearer to the metropolis than any other sea-side place on the south coast, except Brighton. The bathing is excellent in many respects. At low water and the first flow of the tide, bathers may go out a considerable distance without finding the water too deep. But at all times of the tide bathers have the advantage of perfectly pure and translucent sea water; though as the tide rises, it is impossible, except to swimmers, to go far from the machines. The waves, breaking on the shingle, make it necessary that bathers should be careful; but it says much for the safety of the place that up to the present time no fatal accident has ever been known to occur to bathers, whether inhabitants or visitors. Besides sea bathing, there is the accommodation of hot and cold sea-water baths at the Bath-house fronting the sea. For the benefit of invalids, comfortable lodgings, with necessary attendance, can be had on the premises.

The Future of Seaford.—The improvement of the town during the last few years gives fair promise of progress in the future. First the new schools were built; then the parish church was restored; then came the railway, and next the town was supplied with gas. Building has gone on to such an extent that at least twenty-five per cent has been added to the number of inhabited houses. A number of the old houses in the town have been added to or improved. When the raising of the Common and Beamlands, in front of the town—now going on—has been completed, Seaford will possess above thirty acres of pleasure and recreation ground, in the form of a park or public garden. The whole of the top of the beach or full will be converted into an esplanade, with terraces of handsome houses looking on the beach. It may reasonably be hoped that eventually a ride or drive will extend on the top of the full as far as Newhaven. Round the skirt of the ground in front of the town, from the Cliff-end to nearly the western limit of Seaford, houses are to be built, and almost the whole of the land to the west and north of the town has been laid out for wide streets, all giving side or front views of the Sea. It is believed that, in less than twenty years, Seaford will be among the handsomest and healthiest watering places in the kingdom.

History.—An erroneous notion was formerly prevalent that Seaford was the *Civitas Anderida* of the Romans, but the identification of Pevensey with that station has deprived it of all claims to such honour. Sufficient proof, however, of Roman occupation here can be adduced. About three quarters of a mile eastward of the town, on the cliff, are remains of an extensive earthwork, locally called the Roman Camp. Its outlines are tolerably well defined, though it is difficult to ascertain its original extent, as much of its south side has been destroyed by the gradual encroachments of the sea. It has been attributed to the reign of Vespasian. About 45 years since, the remains of a Roman cemetery were discovered at a place called "Green Street," on the estate of the Harison family. Many fine sepulchral urns in a perfect state, filled with the ashes of human bodies, were exhumed, and several of them are now in the possession of F. Sheppard, Esq., of Folkington Place, a few miles distant. More recently, coins of Hadrian, Pius, and Antonia, the daughter of Mark Antony, have been found. The last-mentioned, which is of the purest gold, has the legend "Augusta Antonia—sacerdos Divi Augusti." Although Seaford is not the Anderida of Roman times, it has been plausibly considered to be the *Mercredesburn* of the Saxon Chronicle, where a great battle took place between Ælla, the founder of the Anglo-Saxon kingdom of Sussex and the Britons.*

The first actual mention of Seaford, *eo nomine*, is in the "Acta Sanctorum." A lady of British descent, Lewinna, virgin and martyr, had been slain by the Pagan Saxons for her adherence to the Christian faith, and her remains had

* See Sussex Archæological Collections. Vol. VII.. v. 75.

been deposited in a church, or monastery, dedicated to St. Andrew. In the year 1058, Balgerus, a monk of Bergue St. Winox, near Dunkirk, who had come to England for the purpose of collecting saintly relics, contrived, in a most pious manner, to steal her bones out of the church.* After many perils of the sea, Balgerus had landed at a port called *Sefordt* —not (as I have elsewhere had occasion to remark) at the old port of Seaford, but at Cuckmere haven, two miles and a half eastward, the present geographical boundary of the parish. The church in which the precious relics were deposited, I have conjectured to be that of Alfriston, which is still dedicated to St. Andrew. Many miracles were wrought by these old bones during their conveyance in holy triumph through the towns of Belgium to Bergue, now known as Mons. There they remained for a long while; but were at last destroyed by fire, and other casualties, until at length, in 1522, the sole remnant was a single rib, enclosed in a cotton bag. A very long-winded account of the abstraction of the relics of St. Lewinna is given by the Bollandists, under date of July 24th, of which a summary is printed by Mr. Blaauw, in the first volume of the Sussex Archæological Collections.†

The river Ouse would appear at this period, and earlier, to have taken the *alias* of "Saforda;" for in the eighth century Bertoaldus, a great Sussex Duke, granted Rotherfield and other places in the county to the Abbey of St. Denis, near Paris, the resting-place of many French monarchs. Rother-

* At this period the great rage for the acquisition of relics caused "the end to sanctify the means," and numerous instances of purloining the bones of saints are on record.
† See also my "Worthies of Sussex," p. 317.

field is not strictly on the Ouse, yet a considerable stream rising on the southern confines of that Wealden parish, and flowing past Uckfield, forms the principal tributary of the river; and Rotherfield is described as *super fluvium Saforda*.

Seaford is not mentioned in Domesday Book, either among the possessions of William de Warenne, the Conqueror's son-in-law, or among those of his half-brother, the Earl of Moreton, who held respectively in the Rapes of Lewes and Pevensey. Ultimately, however, it became part of the possessions of the great Earls of Warenne, Lords of Lewes, their *caput baroniæ*, and so continued until the reign of Edward III. After their extinction it belonged to the Lords Poynings, afterwards to the Mowbrays, the Fitz-Alans, and their heritors, the Howards. James I. gave it to William Parker, Lord Mounteagle, in consequence of good service rendered to him by that nobleman, probably in connection with the discovery of Guy Fawkes and the gunpowder plot. The last court of which I find any notice was held in 1603 by Sir Wm. Gratwick, who resided at the Place, or Manor House, subsequently mentioned. Part of the demesne, together with the manor, or reputed manor, of Seaford, was purchased a few years since by Dr. Tyler Smith. The important manor of Chyngton (*vulgo* "Chinting") belonged to the baronial house of De Aquila, Lords of the Rape of Pevensey. Under them a family, who took their surname from the parish (De Saford) held half a knight's fee in this place in the reign of King John.

King John, in one of his hurried journeys through Sussex, passing from Canterbury to Winchester, spent the night of May 23rd, 1216, in this town. Many years later, his son,

Henry III., in May, 1264, passed through Seaford on his way to Lewes, where on the 14th of May, the sanguinary battle took place between that truce-breaking monarch and Simon, Earl of Montfort and Leicester, the leader of the confederate Barons.

The Port. The modern visitor to Seaford may well ask what the inhabitants mean by calling the place "the Town and Cinque-Port of Seaford." A few words of explanation are therefore necessary. We have seen that the river Ouse once had its outlet here; but at what period it became attached to the ancient league known as the Cinque-Ports is unknown, though this must have happened as early as the reign of Henry III. (and before the year 1229), when Seaford is mentioned in a document of importance as the chief "limb," or member, of the principal port of Hastings. Soon after this period, when the first regular Parliament was summoned under Edward I., it had the privilege of sending two members, a right which it continued to exercise till the year 1400. There is, however, no evidence of a return from that date until the reign of Charles I., 1640, from which time until the year 1832, when the Reform Act swept away such small and unimportant boroughs as Seaford had, in the lapse of ages, become. It did not lose its municipal privileges, however, and to the present day it is an exempt jurisdiction, governed by a bailiff, jurats, and freemen; but of this more hereafter.

The following are the main facts in the subsequent history of this old town.

In the stirring times of Edward III. it suffered greatly from the incursions of the French, who "corporally wounded and slew" a number of the inhabitants, so that at the taxation made in 1341-2, under what is known as the Nonæ Inquisition, the revenue to the Crown had greatly diminished. In 1348 the town suffered further depopulation from the great pestilence known as the "Black Death," which destroyed nearly one half of the people of England. Then, as misfortunes rarely come singly, it suffered much from a fire, which consumed the greater part of the place, and few towns in the country could have been in a more miserable plight than this was. But there was still a crowning calamity. As if the devastations of foreign invasion, of pestilence, and of fire were insufficient, a neighbouring proprietor, one James Archer, of Alfriston, a small town three or four miles distant, availed himself of the misery of the stricken town to enrich himself by pulling down many of the remaining houses and selling the materials. The last-mentioned grievance, however, was put a stop to by a royal precept of 30th Edward III., and James Archer's mischievous proceedings were stayed.

In spite of these repeated visitations, which had threatened the entire destruction of the place, the inhabitants had continued, down to the year 1347, to contribute their quota of five ships and eighty mariners to the Cinque-Ports' navy—then the principal naval defence of the realm.

At a later date in the 14th century, when the great family of De Warenne, the feudal lords of Seaford, had become extinct, Michael, Lord Poynings, came into possession, and it would appear that, in order to raise Seaford from the sad condition into which it had fallen, he contemplated the erection of a NEW TOWN within the boundaries of the parish, on the down overlooking the port of Cuckmere. That the work was actually commenced is pretty satisfactorily proved by the fact that, on Chyngton or Chinting Farm, a spot is distinctly traceable which contains beneath its irregular turf the foundations of a large collection of houses. The scheme appears to have been abandoned; but the place is traditionally known as "Poynings' Town." A finer site for a town cannot be found throughout the entire length of the Sussex coast.

In 1496 Seaford contributed to the muster of archers, billmen, and other soldiers furnished by the mother port of Hastings. In 1544 Henry VIII. confirmed a Charter of Incorporation to this ancient Town and Port. This document, which is in good preservation in the town chest, describes the body-corporate as consisting of one Bailiff and the Commonalty of the Town, Parish, and Borough of Seaford, and acknowledges their exemption from all shires and hundreds—in fact, confirms them in all the privileges enjoyed by the greater Cinque-Ports, as a distinct district. The inhabitants had, however, possessed their charter but a few years, when the alteration of the outlet of the river Ouse, as before stated, necessitated the abandonment of Seaford as a port of trade.

In addition to this loss, the town was destined to still further misfortunes. In 1545, the French again landed here, with the intention of burning and sacking the place, but Sir Nicholas Pelham, a direct ancestor of the Earl of Chichester, assisted by the townsmen, and by other landed proprietors of the district, offered so stout a resistance to the invaders that they were fain to sheer off. The quaint epitaph on Sir Nicholas in the church of St. Michael, Lewes, punningly informs us that—

"What time the French sought to have sack'd *Sea-Foord*,
This Pelham did re-*pel-'em* back aboord!"

The subsequent history of Seaford presents us with few

incidents of interest. After the restitution to it of electoral rights in the 17th century, it became one of the most corrupt of "rotten boroughs," and thus, almost inevitably, the tone of morals became low, while the material prosperity of the place was gradually deteriorated.

Among the employments of the humbler class of inhabitants was that of *smuggling*, which was largely carried on, and connived at by the wealthier residents. Many a tale might be told of the "working" of brandy, and hollands, and silk, and tobacco, in the bay and under the cliffs, and of many a sharp rencontre between smuggling lugger and revenue cutter. The Seafordians of those days were also much addicted to the inhuman practice of *wrecking*. Numbers of unfortunate ships were cast away on this coast, and the townsmen looked upon the cargoes as so many "godsends" to them, mercilessly pillaging the hapless crews and owners. That the poorer inhabitants should have been guilty of this crime is not so much a matter of wonder, when we are assured that Mr. Elphick, a leading inhabitant and magistrate, procured seven pipes of sack in this manner; and even Mr. Hide, the minister of the town, and his three sons were suspected of having secreted £300 in money, procured from a wine ship! Eighteen other wreckers of Seaford were accused of minor thefts. Mr. Chowne, a magistrate's son, whose descendants have until recently held property in Seaford, was particularly active in these depredations.* This was in the former half of the 17th century; but things did not greatly improve in the next hundred years. The rapacity of the townspeople in

* *See* Sussex Arch. Coll. Vol. XVII., p. 148.

this respect obtained for them the name of the "*Seaford Shags*," or cormorants.

During the last generation a much better state of things has existed, and the attractions of the town as a watering place have increased. Of its capabilities of improvement in this respect it is unnecessary further to speak. On these the future success of Seaford will mainly depend.

The Municipality. Seaford is a town, parish, and borough of itself, the corporation consisting of a bailiff, jurats, and a commonalty of freemen. It is exempt from all county jurisdiction, and has its own recorder, coroner, and town-clerk. The subordinate officers are a serjeant-at-mace, two chamberlains, a constable, and a headborough. In its diminutive Town-hall courts of assembly and quarter and petty sessions are held. Minor offences are tried, but graver ones are referred to the assizes and quarter-sessions at Lewes. Beneath the town-hall is a prison, which seldom contains an inmate. The bailiff is annually elected on Michaelmas day with certain ancient formalities. A procession, consisting of the officers and freemen, sets out from the "Old Tree" Inn, and the court having been formally opened at the town-hall, the freemen retire in a body to a certain gate-post near West House, where they elect their chief officer for the ensuing year —the magistrates remaining meanwhile in the hall. The records in the town chest contain entries of many criminal and civil causes. Capital punishments were formerly carried out near a place called Hangman's Acre, and the pillory, ducking-stool, stocks, and other similar punishments were not unfrequently resorted to. The site of the pillory was where the "Old Tree" now stands. Many curious extracts from the records, together with a roll of the bailiffs from the year 1541, are given in my previous and larger publication,* which is now out of print. That Seaford was formerly a market-town is shewn by the Records. The market was held on the triangular green called the Crouch, from a cross which formerly stood there.

Ecclesiastical Affairs.—There is a long-preserved tradition that Seaford formerly contained five, or, as some will have it, seven churches. Seaford proper had, however, only one parish, though that one has long been ecclesiastically incorporated with Sutton, the benefice being known as *Sutton cum Seaford*. At the present day Sutton, which lies about half a mile to the N.W. of the town, contains, besides the manorial residence, only three or four houses. Both this and Chyngton are now reputed *vills* of Seaford, and their names are inscribed on the corporate seal. Sutton and Seaford are both *corpora* of prebends in Chichester Cathedral.

The parish CHURCH is dedicated to St. Leonard, who, though the special patron of forests, has several churches in his honour on this part of the coast where woods do not grow. Until lately, it consisted of a tower, nave, north and south aisles, and a kind of "apartment" at the east end, resembling an inn parlour, with sash windows and shutters complete. But *on a changé tout cela*, and now Seaford can boast of one of the neatest and most tasteful churches in the district. The restorations and additions were made in 1861-2 by the exertions of the late Rev. Jas. Carnegie, the vicar, aided by liberal subscriptions; and the architect was the late John Billing, Esq.

The tower, which remains in *statu quo*, is built in three

* "Memorials of the Town, Parish, and Cinque-Port of Seaford, Historical and Antiquarian." London, 1855. A copy of this little volume can be seen at most of the lodging-houses and inns.

stages diminishing upwards. The material is sandstone and cut flint. On the middle stage is a "cross Calvary" worked in flint. The other features of the building are in various styles, Norman, Early-English, and later. Mr. Billing's additions consist of two short transepts, and a handsome chancel, with a polygonal termination. There are handsome memorial windows for members of the families of Carnegie, Harison, Simmons, Hincks, Pearce, &c. There are also various tablets and slabs to the memory of local families. A musical peal of eight bells adds to the attractions of the church.

The nave of the older portion of the building is separated from the aisles by pointed arches, with cylindrical columns and Transition-Norman capitals. The arches have recessed mouldings of peculiar character, with a kind of rib of two square members under the soffit. Over the apex of each arch is a pointed clerestory window. The capital of the column opposite the principal entrance is sculptured with representations of the Baptism, the Crucifixion, &c. A rudely-carved representation of St. Michael and the Dragon was found many years since in digging a grave, and fixed in its present position near this capital. The parish register commences in 1558, and contains some interesing entries. The Vicarage is in the gift of the Lord Chancellor, and the present incumbent is the Rev. W. H. M. Buck.

As to the other churches of the town, that of Sutton is, doubtless, one of the reputed five. Its foundations are still traceable near Sutton Place. The other three appear to have been the following:—

1. The church or chapel of St. James, attached to the Hospital of Lepers, formerly situated in the deep dell to the north of the town on the road to Blatchington. This build-

ing disappeared at the Reformation, though its site is still pointed out. Of the foundation of this Hospital, little is known. The first record of it extant is a grant, by Roger Ashurst, or Ashgrove (De Fraxineto), in 1172, of seven acres of land to the establishment. The original deed, with its seal of white wax, is deposited in the Museum at Lewes Castle. In the reign of Queen Elizabeth (157—) the site and lands became the property of Mary, Countess of Pembroke, celebrated by Ben Jonson, in the well-known epitaph:

> "Underneath this marble hearse,
> Lies the subject of all verse:
> Sydney's sister, Pembroke's mother,
> Death, ere thou hast slain another,
> Fair, and learned, and good as she,
> Time shall throw a dart at thee!"

The land was afterwards held on lease successively by the families of Elphick and Chambers, of the prebend of Bargham, in Chichester Cathedral.

2. In an old Corporation record mention is made of "Church-lands on the hill." This has been interpreted to mean that a church once stood there; it may, however, simply signify land forming part of the glebe of St. Leonard's. There was a *Hermitage* on the cliff, in 1272, when the Hermit, named Peter, obtained letters of protection for five years. The cell of that recluse probably had its chapel, by courtesy called a church.*

---

* A friend stands out for the actual existence of a considerable church on the Down, basing his argument upon a record in the corporation chest, temp. Charles I., to the effect that every inhabitant might "keep a cowe or more there," until 6s. 8d. were paid to the use of the "church there." This was a deposition made by the *Vicar of Seaford* at the period. The Harison family pay a rent to the corporation in respect of two acres of land on the Down, which my friend thinks the site of the supposed ancient church and churchyard. There certainly was no church there so late as the time of the Stuarts. Hundreds of fields, &c., are called "church lands," "church fields," &c., which were merely outlying pieces of glebe.

3. The manor of Chyngton, about one mile eastward of the town, was an early appendage to the priory of Michelham, in Sussex, and had a Chapel.

These five ecclesiastical foundations, then, may have all popularly ranked as churches, and at least two or three of them were really so. Indeed, there may have been a *sixth*, represented by a vaulted apartment in a garden in Church Street, the property of Robertson Griffiths, Esq. *See plate II.*

This ancient Crypt (which has over it a building called "The Folly," now used as a cottage) is 27ft. 3in. long; 13ft. 4in. wide; and 11ft. 4in. high. The vaulting ribs are simple, and the bosses at the intersection of Early English character. There are two approaches to it from the ground level, by steps. It is now undergoing restoration, and is one of the most interesting relics of ancient Seaford.[*] There is another vaulted apartment beneath the Plough Inn, in the same street, and over it a room which contains a chimney-piece of ancient date. *See plate II.*

Sutton was anciently, as we have seen, a separate parish. It had two manors, Sutton-Sandore, and Sutton-Peverel. The former belonged to William de Abrincis, who, being one of the barons in arms again King John, was imprisoned and mulcted in a heavy sum, to raise which he sold this manor to the Abbot and Convent of Robertsbridge. In the reign of Henry VIII., it was held on lease by John Seman, ancestor of one of the numerous Seaford families now called Simmons. It was afterwards held by the family of Elphick, and from

[*] According to tradition, the court house or town-hall of Seaford formerly stood over this crypt. The date of the present town-hall is not known.

PLATE II.

CRYPT, SEAFORD.

MANTEL-PIECE, PLOUGH INN, SEAFORD.

them it passed, by marriage, in the seventeenth century, to the family of Harison, the present owners. Sutton-Peverel received its suffix from the great Norman family of that name, who also held Blatchington. In the fifteenth century it belonged to the Lords de la Warr, and at a later date to the family of Chowne. It is now the property of Dr. Tyler Smith.

Chyngton or *Chinting* manor forms the eastern part of the parish, and is bounded on the east by the river Cuckmere. It belonged in Norman times to the great family of De Aquila, who gave it, *temp.* Henry III., to the priory of Michelham. The brethren of that house established here a *grange* with a chapel. Some Early-English remains were disclosed, during alterations in the house a few years since. The estate has belonged for many generations to the noble family of Pelham, the Earl of Chichester being the present owner.

The local influence of the De Aquilas here is still shewn by the Corporation seal, which has on the obverse an eagle, with the words SIGILLVM BURGENSIVM DE SAFFORDIA. On the reverse, which is of more modern date, is an antique ship, allusive to Cinque-Port privileges, and the quaint legend in mixed Latin and English—"WITH SUTTONII ÆT CHYNGTON."

I must not close my account of Sutton and Chyngton without mentioning that there is, at the verge of the lofty cliffs, at the point where the two estates meet, a place known by the mysterious and fairy-like name of "Puck-Church Parlour." A gap, or hollow descent to the sea, similar to Hope Gap, Birling Gap, &c., formerly existed here; but the inroads of the ocean have rendered the cliff inaccessible from below. A little to the westward of the remains of the gap there is a rough and narrow pathway from the top of the cliff, leading downwards a distance (measured perpendicularly) of about ten yards, in front of the precipice, to three platforms, each a few yards square, to which the above romantic designation is attached. At what period the King of the Fairies built his Church, and occupied his Parlour, it would be vain to conjecture, but the place is evidently connected with some ancient local superstition. At present, human feet rarely venture to tread the perilous approach to these romantic ledges, the fee simple being enjoyed by a pair or two of old foxes, which find here a most secure retreat from dog and hunter, and are occasionally visited in their elevated abode by the chough, the raven, the sea-gull, and the peregrine falcon. The last named noble bird occasionally breeds in the cliff. It is much prized by ornithologists, and the current price for a fledgling is a guinea.

Millburgh, the property of John Purcell Fitzgerald, Esq., has the *aliases* of "Corsica Hall," and "The Lodge." It is an excellent mansion, and stands on an eminence eastward of the town. A mill formerly stood here, whence the name, and some cannons occupied this commanding position.

The house was originally built at Ringmer, near Lewes, by a person named Whitfield, who was a great smuggler of Corsican wine, whence the name Corsica Hall. After his death, it was occupied by Francis, fifth Lord Napier, and in the month of May, 1772, became the scene of a painful domestic tragedy. One of his lordship's sons, a little boy, one day in a frolicsome humour, took up a loaded pistol that had been inadvertently left upon a table at which the Rev. Mr. Loudon, his lordship's domestic chaplain and private tutor, was sitting, and, aiming it at him, said, "Shall I shoot you?" The reverend gentleman, thinking the pistol empty, laughingly replied, "Shoot on!" The child pulled the trigger, the discharge took place, and Mr. Loudon fell dead upon the floor. From this tragical event, Corsica Hall was invested by the ignorant and superstitious with an evil and unlucky character; and after the death of Lord Napier, no tenant could be found for it. It was, therefore, pulled down and purchased by a clockmaker of Lewes, named Harben, who, according to popular rumour, had become suddenly rich by buying, as base metal, some of the golden spoils of the celebrated wreck of the " Nympha Americana," which took place near Beachy Head some years previously. However this may have been, Mr. Harben removed Corsica Hall to its present site, resided in it in good style, and became a person of leading influence in the political affairs of the borough.

Seaford formerly boasted of several excellent houses; but some of them have been destroyed, or have gone to decay. On the east side of Broad Street stood *Hurdis House*, a large mansion with a cupola and open gallery. It was named after its proprietors, a family intimately connected with Seaford in the last century.* *Seaford House*, in the eastern part of the town, belonged to the great legal celebrity, Sir John Leach, who was M.P. for the town in 1802, and from whom it passed to Charles Rose Ellis, Esq., created in 1826 BARON SEAFORD. It is now the property of Lord Howard de Walden and Sea-

* Part of the site is now occupied by the residence of B. J. Tuck, Esq.

ford. It will interest every reader to know that it was in this house that Tennyson wrote his ode on the funeral of the Duke of Wellington. Canning often ate and dined in this house when Prime Minister. *Place House*, in Broad Street, a structure of flint with projecting wings, was originally a handsome mansion: it is now occupied by cottagers. It was the residence of the ancient Sussex family of Gratwicke, having been built by Sir William Gratwicke and Lady Margery, his wife, whose initials, with the date 1603, are over the front door. Sir William was Lord of the Manor of Seaford in that year. There are other good family residences, which we have not space to describe.

Military Defences.—The Martello Tower, No. 74, the westernmost of the series, stands on the beach opposite the south-eastern quarter of the town. Like its brethren, it is a low circular structure, with a wide moat, and drawbridge, and mounts one swivel cannon. It is now almost useless.* To the west of this is a battery constructed for four guns (68 and 32-pounders.) This was overturned, and became a complete wreck by the great inundation of 1865. There were formerly other small forts on Millburgh and at the Cliff end; and the spot called West Gun, at the western extremity of the town, marks the site of a piece of ordnance. This may be the proper place to speak of the

Encroachments of the Sea and Inundations. The heavy set of the tides from the south-west, during storms blowing from that quarter, have, on several occasions, placed the lower portion of the town in some jeopardy. The lengthening of

* It cost the enormous sum of £18,000, and contains, besides a magazine, apartments for an officer and 24 men.

the piers, and the erection of strong groynes at Newhaven, have had the effect of driving the tidal waves with a stronger *ictus* on the Seaford end of the Bay. This led some years ago to many shipwrecks. In 1809 seven merchantmen were driven ashore during a violent gale, with the loss of the vessels and thirty-one men. Various measures have been adopted to remedy the evil. In 1850 an attempt was made, by blasting an immense mass of the chalk cliff into the sea, to form a kind of rough groyne. The explosion, which was carried out by a body of Sappers and Miners, was successful enough, but too much gunpowder being used, the chalk dislodged was reduced to small pieces, and the force of the tides soon swept away the enormous mole, which consisted of many thousands of tons; and the labour and expense were lost. A groyne of timber lately erected close to the Cliff-end promises to be more successful, as it has already had the effect of considerably augmenting the body of shingle on the "full," thus protecting the low ground lying immediately in front of the lower part of the town. We may, therefore, reasonably hope that we shall have no more inundations like that below mentioned.

On November 23rd, 1824, there occurred a very violent storm and high tide. The sea broke its accustomed bounds near the Martello Tower, and bursting through the "full" of the beach, swept with resistless fury across the Beamlands, deluging the lower portion of the town, while another breach of vast magnitude was made to the westward, near Blatchington Battery. The inundation commenced soon after eleven o'clock, a.m., which was more than an hour after the regular time of high water. The water forced its way into several of the houses, to a depth of almost six feet, so that the alarmed inhabitants had to make their escape from the chamber windows by the aid of boats, which were rowed some little distance up two or three of the main streets. Fishing-boats, driven from their moorings, were dashed ashore, and one of large size was lifted by the billows into the enclosure called the Little Steyne, while others were carried over flint walls to a great distance from the sea. A barge was driven up the Bishopston valley, almost as far as Norton, and deposited in a grove of elm trees, thus almost realizing Horace's—

"Piscium et summa genus hæsit *ulmo*, Nota quæ sedes fuerat columbis;"

whilst in another direction the waves flowed to Blatchington Pond, more than half a mile from high-water mark. Some poultry, which had taken refuge upon a hay-stack, were floated in safety to a spot five hundred yards from that from whence they had set sail. Providentially there was no loss of life or limb, and little mischief occurred beyond the destruction of a few cottages and buildings of small value. The next tide was restrained within its ordinary limits, and no similar inroad of Father Neptune took place for about forty years. In the winters of 1865 and 1866 there were considerable inundations, but with no very damaging results.

The *Drainage* of Seaford, which is on the most approved modern principles, is equal if not superior to that of any watering-place on the South Coast. It was designed by Messrs. Gotto and Beesley, the eminent sanitary engineers. Their plan consists of glazed stoneware pipes laid through all the streets, the owner of every house being compelled by law to drain his house properly. These pipes all converge to a barrel sewer, more than six feet in circumference, which, commencing near Marine Terrace, runs from thence in an easterly direction in front of the town, along the carriage road past Millburgh, or Corsica Hall (now used as a Convalescent Hospital) to the Cliff End, where a pipe is carried through the beach to a point not far from the groyne, and beyond low water mark; so that the extremity of the pipe will always be covered with water. It is also arranged that the sewage will be discharged when the tide is receding towards the ebb, at which time a current sets to the eastward, towards Beachy Head, carrying the contents of the sewer out to sea far away from the town. The outlet of the sewer is thus at a considerable distance from the houses, the new bathing place, and the parts of the beach most frequented; but, to prevent the possibility of any unpleasantness arising, a plan has been adopted for deodorizing the sewage before it is discharged into the sea.

The engineers have also introduced an ingenious system of flushing; a large tank, capable of containing eighteen thousand gallons, being placed at the western extremity of the town, near Telsemaure House. This reservoir fills itself from the sea at every high tide, and the large volume of clean water collected being suddenly discharged when the tide is receding, washes the sewer out thoroughly twice in every twenty-four hours; and thus prevents the possibility of any accumulations. The sewers are ventilated by numerous openings, guarded by charcoal ventilators. This arrangement prevents the accumulation of noxious gases, and deodorizes the air of the sewers as it escapes.

The old pebble gutters, which were formerly so offensive and inconvenient, have been replaced by brick channels. The "black ditch," near the Tower, which had an unenviable notoriety, will soon become a matter of history.

The works are so constructed, that at any future time, if it should be thought desirable, the sewage may be disposed of for the purposes of irrigation.*

The Fishery.—Seaford Bay abounds in fish of many kinds, as soles, whiting, gurnets, plaice, mackerel, herrings, conger, skate, gar, sprats, mullet, brill, &c. At times, crabs and lobsters are plentiful; but the chief delicacy taken here is the prawn, and for this Seaford is widely renowned.† As a large proportion of the poorer classes subsist by the dangerous pursuit of fishing, it is most desirable that something should be done to improve their position, and to enable them to compete with the fishermen of more favoured towns. Fishing boats come from Brighton, Hastings, Eastbourne, &c., and carry off the spoils which seem naturally to belong to Seaford. The fishermen feel this, and attribute their want of prosperity to the defect of length in their boats. They say that if they had 20 or 22 foot boats instead of the 18 foot ones now in use, they could greatly increase their trade, the shorter boat being unable to encounter the rough seas which so often prevail in the bay. It is thought that if a few enterprising individuals would raise the necessary funds, and appoint an experienced superintendent, a large and profitable fishery might be carried on.

* This notice of the sewerage has been kindly communicated by B. J. Tuck, Esq., M.R.C.S.
† Mackerel are caught in Seine nets. Visitors derive much amusement from prawning on the rocks.

Charities, Education, &c. ALMSHOUSES were founded in 1858, by the liberality of John Purcell Fitzgerald, Esq., for poor men and women who, besides comfortable apartments, receive a small weekly stipend. The almshouses form a neat brick building, near the north side of the town, in Old Chapel Lane. The income is derived from certain houses in the town, and is administered by trustees. The inmates are elected from a district, the limits of which are a radius of nine miles. The foundation stone was laid July 21st, 1864.

THE SEA-SIDE CONVALESCENT HOSPITAL was established in 1860, for the purpose of affording sea air and bathing to poor persons, who, from confinement in the sick wards of hospitals, or in the often more prejudicial atmosphere of their own homes, are unable to regain the strength necessary to permit them to resume their employment. The hospital provides for these sufferers efficient domestic arrangements under the care of a matron, and a supply of good and wholesome nourishment. No cases which could possibly convey infection to the other inmates, or to the inhabitants of the neighbourhood, are admitted; and separate baths are provided for their special use.

The number of inmates varies with circumstances. In 1866, 313 patients enjoyed the advantages of this charity. They are at present located in the mansion called Millburgh, or Corsica Hall, previously mentioned, which, from its proximity to the sea and to the health-inspiring downs behind it, is remarkably well adapted to the purpose. A medical officer (T. F. Sanger, Esq.) visits the establishment twice a week.

THE NATIONAL SCHOOLS are supported in the usual

mode, under the management of the Vicar of the parish and a committee. The building, which is well adapted to its purpose, stands a little to the eastward of the town.* Attached to the Independent Chapel, under the care of the Rev. Edwin Green, in East Street, is a large and commodious school-room, recently erected by the liberality of Thos. Crook, Esq. There is an Infant School in Old Chapel Lane.

Sports and Amusements. Seaford offers many facilities to the lover of out-door recreations. Pleasure boats may be had, and from these angling for many of the varieties of fish which the bay affords, enjoyed. The neighbouring river Cuckmere produces sport for the experienced disciple of Izaak Walton. The Hunting of the district is remarkably good. The South Down Fox-hounds frequently meet at and near the town; and the Eastbourne and Brookside Harriers are within a very easy distance. A good training establishment for race-horses exists at Alfriston, about three miles distant. Cricket is much cultivated here, on an excellent ground, and the "Seaford Eleven" are always ready to welcome visitors to the sport.

Walks and Drives. Although Seaford cannot, as yet, boast of any public promenades, like those furnished by the more important watering places, it possesses abundance of facilities for walking and for horse and carriage exercise. A stroll on the beach is very agreeable, and there is every opportunity of watching the various phases of sea scenery. This year an attempt to convert the top of the "full," or beach, into a promenade has been made.

* The building was erected at the expense of J. P. Fitzgerald, Esq., on land presented by the Earl of Chichester.

One of the first objects that attract the notice of a stranger is the swelling Down to the eastward, which, with its chalk cliffs, presents itself romantically to the view of the town. The hill rises abruptly from the flat land below, and is covered with a fine turf, overgrown here and there with bushes of dark green furze, with their golden blossoms. A foot-path, leading past the Convalescent Hospital, brings the pedestrian at once to the Down. In ascending this height he will naturally "pull up," in order to take breath, and by the instinct which always governs people who walk up hill, he will turn round. Then he will behold one of the most charming scenes on the southern coast. The Bay, with its sweep of several miles, in its various phases of ocean calm and billow; the opposite cliffs of Newhaven, with steamers and sailing craft approaching or leaving the harbour; the low lands in the foreground, flanked by the cheerful-looking town, with its old grey church in the middle distance; more to the right the picturesque village and church of Blatchington, embosomed in trees, and a grey background of hills stretching away to Mount Harry, behind Lewes—form, in the *ensemble*, a picture of no ordinary interest or beauty.*
Ascending the undulating Down, we reach traces of the embankments of the ROMAN CAMP referred to heretofore, and passing on, reach the highest point of Seaford Cliff. Continuing the walk across the ever-varying sweeps of turf, we catch sight of the undulated cliffs of pure white, which, from their number, are called the "Seven Sisters," presenting a most striking aspect. We reach, at somewhat more than

* Brighton, Worthing, and Highdown Hill may be seen in clear weather, and occasionally the Isle of Wight.

two miles from the Cliff-end, the valley of the CUCKMERE, which winds its sluggish course through a broad alluvial valley towards the sea. Glancing in the direction of the course of the river, towards the north, we see the old church and town of Alfriston, and beyond it, in the far distance, a peep of the great Weald, a beautiful "bit" of the picturesque. The return walk may be varied by going abruptly to the left, and so reaching the town by way of Chyngton and Green Street.

A short and agreeable walk is that to BLATCHINGTON and BISHOPSTON, two neighbouring villages. Leaving the town by Broad Street, the pedestrian soon reaches an abrupt turn in the road near Cinque-Port Place, and the gas works in a deep dell on the left. Near this spot stood the old hospital of St. James. Further on, near a pond, the road takes another sharp turn northwards, and the village of Blatchington is soon reached. It is picturesquely situated amidst trees, and commands a beautiful view over Seaford and the Channel. The church is well worthy of attention, not only for the general symmetry of its form, but for some peculiarity of detail well worthy of the attention of the ecclesiologist. It has features of Norman, early English, and subsequent styles. The churchyard is remarkable for its neat and elegant arrangements; during the summer months it is a perfect garden, the graves being planted with flowers of every hue. This attention is due to the care and taste of the rector, the Rev. R. N. Dennis, and his wife. Blatchington Court is the residence of Dr. Tyler Smith, and stands in agreeable grounds on the left. Passing the church, a road turns at a right angle westward, and at a short distance a footpath on the right leads by an up and down course of 1¼ mile to BISHOPSTON, a small village amidst beautiful trees. The venerable little church contains some very remarkable features, some of which are unquestionably Saxon, especially the south porch, which has a sun-dial with the name EADRIC on it. Beyond the chancel is an addition, probably a Ladye chapel, but which has been designated by some a " sanctum-sanctorum." There are a few interesting memorials; and among the modern ones, a tablet to Dr. Hurdis, Professor of Poetry at Oxford, and the friend of Cowper and Hayley. He was rector of this parish, and resided here in quietude, printing at his private press his own poems, " The Village Curate," and many others, which were very popular in their day, and playing his favourite little organ, which, by the kindness of his son, James Henry Hurdis, an eminent amateur engraver, is now in the possession of the writer of these lines. The great political Duke of Newcastle had a large mansion at this place, which was destroyed many years since. Further up the valley is Norton, a picturesque hamlet, the name of which seems to be a correlative of Sutton in Seaford. The return walk may be made by Blatchington Fort.

NEWHAVEN may be reached by three routes. The first is by railway, which occupies a few minutes only; the second by a very circuitous carriage-road, the engineer of which must have been actuated by the principle that " one good *turn* deserves another;" and the third, and most interesting, by a combination of roadway and footpath. Leaving the southern part of the town, the pedestrian passes by Telsemaure House, and arrives at Blatchington Fort, a battery mounted with six heavy guns. There were formerly extensive barracks at this spot; and the fort is still used by the Sussex Artillery Militia, the Cinque-Port Volunteers, &c. A coastguard station is fixed here, under the command of a Lieutenant. Further on, passing a wayside inn, called the Buckle, we reach a causeway, which brings us, in a few minutes, to Bishopston TIDE-MILLS, the establishment of Messrs. Catt. This is one of the most extensive works of the kind in the south of England. The houses connected with them form a kind of colony, and include a pleasant residence, with beautiful gardens, a conservatory, &c. The late Mr. William Catt, the proprietor, was intimately acquainted with King Louis Philippe, and very near to these mills it was the fortune of that dethroned monarch to land in 1848, Mr. Catt being the first to hail and welcome him to the safety of British soil. A very short walk brings us to Newhaven Wharf, the station from which, once a day in winter, and twice in summer, excellent steamers start for Dieppe. This route (*viâ* Newhaven and Dieppe) from London to Paris is by far the shortest, and is often accomplished in 12 or 14 hours. There is a large hotel for the accommodation of travellers. The town of Newhaven consists mainly of one street, which leads to the Brighton road. The Church is well worthy of inspection; the nave, &c., are recent, but the tower at the east end, with its little apsidal termination of early Norman date, affords an agreeable study for the lover of old churches. Newhaven has a very considerable coasting trade. On the heights to the west of the harbour, there are traces of a Roman camp corresponding with that on Seaford heights; and here is in course of erection a very strong fort, for the protection of Seaford Bay. It will mount, when finished, 75 guns, and contain accommodation for 300 men. The works may be visited by tourists, and the west pier, close by, forms an agreeable promenade. Refections may be had at the London and Paris Hotel, on the wharf; and also at the Bridge Hotel, where King Louis Philippe and his Queen passed the first night after their arrival on these shores.

If visitors wish to extend their excursions, they may on their arrival at Newhaven, by rail, follow the course of the Ouse, by what is called the BROOKSIDE, a series of villages on the west side of the river. These are Piddinghoe, a straggling village, with a curious little round-towered church; Southease, with a still smaller round-towered church;* Rodmell, a picturesque village, with a church of considerable interest, and a wayside inn. Further on are Iford on the right, and Kingston on the left, with interesting churches.

LEWES, eight miles from Newhaven by road, and six by rail, should also be visited. This old county-town, with 10,000 inhabitants, has many points of interest, and will amply repay a visit. The principal points of interest are the ruins of the Priory, founded by Gundrada, daughter of William the Conqueror, and her husband, William de Warenne, whose remains were discovered in 1845, and now lie in a beautiful little sacellum in the church of Southover, hard by; Lewes Castle with its Barbican, Keep, and Archæological Museum; and the monument of Magnus, a Danish Prince, at St. John's Church. Beyond the town is Mount

* There are but three of these rare churches in Sussex, the third being that of St. Michael, at Lewes.

Harry, the scene of the memorable battle of Lewes, 1264, between Henry the Third and the confederated barons, under Simon de Montfort. The scenery around Lewes is every way romantic and beautiful. The geologist should visit the Combe and Southerham chalk-pits.

BEACHY HEAD AND BELTOUT.—This is a rather laborious excursion, and requires a well-appointed vehicle. The distance is, as the crow flies, about six miles. The route is by Sutton, Excete bridge (near which is West Dean, with an interesting church and a parsonage house nearly intact, dating from the 14th century), then up a steep hill to Friston Mill and Church, leaving on the left, in a deep valley, Friston Place, a mansion of the 14th century, but modernized in the 17th. The view is romantic and agreeable. The descent of the hill brings us to the pleasant village of East Dean. Following this *dean*, or valley, to Birling farm, we ascend another acclivity, and passing the lighthouse of Beltout and its ancient earthwork, at length reach Beachy head. This bold promontory it is difficult to describe. It rises to the great height of 575 feet, and has for its sea-front an immense perpendicular cliff of pure white chalk. Here and there irregular crags of the same material stand out in half-detached masses, which, as well as the sea, may be viewed obliquely from different points near the edge of the cliff. Inland the prospect is charmingly bold and diversified. Beachy Head has an unfavourable reputation for the number of shipwrecks which formerly took place beneath its frowning heights; but the erection of the lighthouse at Beltout has rendered these calamities extremely rare. To record the various facts connected with this well-known promontory—

the great naval victory gained by the Dutch over our fleet in 1690; the losses of life and property by wreck; the hairbreadth escapes of castaway mariners; the perilous descents of the foolhardy; the feats of "willock" shooters; the smuggling; and a score of other matters, would far exceed the limits and design of this little book.

EASTBOURNE is three miles further on; but the Seaford visitor who desires to see that rising watering-place would achieve his object more readily by taking the train *via* Lewes and Polegate.

FIRLE BEACON, one of the loftiest points of the South Downs, lies in a direction nearly due north of Blatchington, and is distant about six miles. It is well adapted for pic-nic parties, and commands the finest imaginable view of the great Weald of Sussex, extending right and left over a vast expanse of country. For this excursion and for Beachy Head wagonettes are the proper mode of conveyance, and these and other carriages can be obtained at the Terminus Hotel. Conveyances are also let at the New Inn, and by several other fly-proprietors in the town.*

An agreeable morning walk or drive may be had to *Littlington* and *Alfriston*, the distance being about four miles. Alfriston is a quaint little town of one short street. It has a cruciform church of very large dimensions, with some

---

* It is much to be regretted that the road to Firle Beacon is not put in order. The right of way to the Beacon and Alciston is exercised by the Seafordians. An old causeway is discernible for great part of the distance, but it has long passed into a condition of impracticable ruts. For this reason carts and carriages have to pass over down and ploughed land. The Seaford charioteers, however, manage the drive with perfect safety, though sometimes with a little more jolting than is quite agreeable. Firle Beacon, with its magnificent panorama, should be the Lion of Seaford as the Devil's Dyke is of Brighton, and this renders it more desirable that the approach to it should be improved.

interesting details in the chancel. A remarkable old inn, of the Tudor period, with curious wood carvings on its front, and a mutilated cross in the street are other objects worthy of attention. On the return it may be worth while to visit the Pleasure-Garden at Littlington, conducted by Mr. F. Russell, where pic-nics may be held, and where tea and more invigorating refreshments can be obtained, and an afternoon agreeably spent. The grounds are spacious, and pleasantly wooded. The ecclesiologist may also be gratified by an inspection of the little parish church, which possesses some interesting features.

A second excursion to Lewes may be made, by carriage, by the right bank of the Ouse, where there are several little villages and churches. Denton, Heighton (now churchless), Tarring, Beddingham—the last remarkable as being mentioned in the will of King Alfred. Concerning three of these small villages there is a local witticism—

> "Heighton, Denton, Tarring,
> All begins with A!"

A *détour* to the right to the village of Firle, enables us to visit a picturesque and well-ordered spot, the principal objects of which are the handsome mansion and park of Lord Viscount Gage, whose ancestors in a long series lie buried within a picturesque monumental church.

The excursions above enumerated may be prolonged in various directions, and visitors will doubtless select for themselves scenes and objects of interest, which have escaped us in this hasty sketch.

Railway Trains.—There are about five departures, and as many arrivals on week days. On Sundays two trains run each way.

Postal Arrangements.—The Post-town is Lewes. The morning mail delivery is about eight o'clock; the next about twelve. Letters can be despatched at 2 p.m., and about 6 p.m., but the times vary. On Sunday morning the arrival is as on week days, and letters must be posted before five. There is a Money-order Office at Seaford.

CPSIA information can be obtained
at www.ICGtesting.com
Printed in the USA
LVIC041435070113

314706LV00004B